# OSTER DIGITAL FRENCH DOOR OVEN COOKBOOK

80 EASY AND MOUTHWATERING OVEN RECIPES. | 30-DAY MEAL PLAN INCLUDED.

PAMELA KENDRICK

# CONTENTS

*Introduction*      ix

## BREAKFAST

1. Apple Oat Cups      3
2. Spinach Tomato Egg Muffins      5
3. Perfect Potato Casserole      7
4. Ham Cheese Casserole      9
5. Fluffy Breakfast Egg Muffins      11
6. Pumpkin Bread      13
7. Healthy Banana Bread      15
8. Baked Oatmeal      17
9. Healthy Oat Muffins      19
10. Baked Cinnamon Oatmeal      21

## POULTRY

11. Juicy Chicken Drumsticks      25
12. Crispy Chicken Wings      27
13. Lemon Pepper Chicken Wings      29
14. Delicious Turkey Cutlets      31
15. Turkey Spinach Patties      33
16. Turkey Meatballs      35
17. Healthy Chicken Fritters      37
18. Creamy Chicken      39
19. Easy Brown Sugar Chicken      41
20. Chicken Meatballs      43

## BEEF, PORK & LAMB

| | |
|---|---|
| 21. Beef Onion Bake | 47 |
| 22. Simple Spiced Pork Chops | 49 |
| 23. Quick Ranch Pork Chops | 51 |
| 24. Pork Chops with Potatoes | 53 |
| 25. Baked Pork Patties | 55 |
| 26. Meatballs | 57 |
| 27. Simple Lamb Patties | 59 |
| 28. Baked Pork Ribs | 61 |
| 29. Juicy Pork Tenderloin | 63 |
| 30. Rosemary Pork Chops | 65 |
| 31. Greek Lamb Patties | 67 |
| 32. Lamb Meatballs | 69 |
| 33. Pork Meatballs | 71 |
| 34. Beef Zucchini Burger Patties | 73 |
| 35. Smoked Paprika Pork Chops | 75 |

## FISH & SEAFOOD

| | |
|---|---|
| 36. Baked Salmon Patties | 79 |
| 37. Simple Cajun Salmon | 81 |
| 38. Tasty Crab Patties | 83 |
| 39. Garlic Butter Shrimp | 85 |
| 40. Sweet Dijon Salmon | 87 |
| 41. Flavorful Shrimp Fajitas | 89 |
| 42. Delicious Pesto Salmon | 91 |
| 43. Garlic Tilapia | 93 |
| 44. Flavors Catfish Fillets | 95 |
| 45. Blackened Fish Fillets | 97 |

## VEGETABLES & SIDE DISHES

| | |
|---|---|
| 46. Parmesan Cauliflower Florets | 101 |
| 47. Zucchini Tomato Bake | 103 |
| 48. Zucchini Potato Gratin | 105 |
| 49. Spinach Zucchini Casserole | 107 |
| 50. Healthy Carrot Fries | 109 |
| 51. Baked Curried Cauliflower Florets | 111 |
| 52. Balsamic Mushrooms | 113 |

| | |
|---|---|
| 53. Cheesy Broccoli Fritters | 115 |
| 54. Creamy Broccoli Casserole | 117 |
| 55. Baked Sweet Potatoes & Apple | 119 |

## SNACKS & APPETIZERS

| | |
|---|---|
| 56. Bacon Jalapeno Poppers | 123 |
| 57. Perfect Crab Dip | 125 |
| 58. Yummy Corn Dip | 127 |
| 59. Garlic Cheese Dip | 129 |
| 60. Baked Potato Wedges | 131 |
| 61. Healthy Vegetable Bites | 133 |
| 62. Tasty Roasted Chickpeas | 135 |
| 63. Cheesy Cauliflower Tots | 137 |

## DEHYDRATE

| | |
|---|---|
| 64. Yellow Squash Chips | 141 |
| 65. Eggplant Chips | 142 |
| 66. Kiwi Chips | 144 |
| 67. Kale Chips | 145 |
| 68. Zucchini Chips | 147 |
| 69. Banana Slices | 149 |
| 70. Pear Slices | 150 |
| 71. Salmon Jerky | 151 |

## DESSERTS

| | |
|---|---|
| 72. Delicious Pineapple Bars | 155 |
| 73. Cinnamon Honey Pears | 157 |
| 74. Cinnamon Apple Slices | 159 |
| 75. Moist Yogurt Cake | 161 |
| 76. Easy Blonde Brownie | 163 |
| 77. Fudgy Chocolate Brownies | 165 |
| 78. Soft & Moist Lemon Brownies | 167 |
| 79. Easy Lemon Cookies | 169 |

80. Chocolate Chip Cookies　　　　　　　　171

30-Day Meal Plan　　　　　　　　173

*Conclusion*　　　　　　　　177

© **Copyright 2021 by Pamela Kendrick. All Rights Reserved.**

In no way is it legal to reproduce, duplicate, or transmit any part of this document by either electronic means or in printed format. Recording of this publication is strictly prohibited, and any storage of this material is not allowed unless with written permission from the publisher. All rights reserved.

The information provided herein is stated to be truthful and consistent, in that any liability, regarding inattention or otherwise, by any usage or abuse of any policies, processes, or directions contained within is the solitary and complete responsibility of the recipient reader. Under no circumstances will any legal liability or blame be held against the publisher for any reparation, damages, or monetary loss due to the information herein, either directly or indirectly.

Respective authors own all copyrights not held by the publisher.

**Legal Notice:**

This book is copyright protected. This is only for personal use. You cannot amend, distribute, sell, use, quote or paraphrase any part of the content within this book without the consent of the author or copyright owner. Legal action will be pursued if this is breached.

**Disclaimer Notice:**

Please note the information contained within this document is for educational and entertainment purposes only. Every attempt has been made to provide accurate, up-to-date and reliable, complete information. No warranties of any kind are expressed or implied. Readers acknowledge that the author is not engaging in the rendering of legal, financial, medical or professional advice.

By reading this document, the reader agrees that under no circumstances are we responsible for any losses, direct or indirect, which are incurred as a result of the use of information contained within this document, including, but not limited to, errors, omissions, or inaccuracies.

# INTRODUCTION

The Oster Digital French door oven is one of the best innovative convection oven loaded with turbo convection technology which makes your daily cooking process faster. The Oster oven is perfect kitchen appliances capable to handle multiple tasks into single appliances. A digital touch control panel helps you to perform different cooking tasks like Bake, Broil, Toast, Warm, Pizza, Defrost, and Dehydrate. It looks attractive and stylish when you pull a single door to open both the door by just one hand pull. One of the best parts of the oven is it comes with extra-large interior space. The two rack position helps to maximize your cooking flexibility. So you can cook whole family food into a single cooking cycle.

    The turbo convection baking technology is one of the innovative cooking functions added to the oven. Using this function you can bake your food faster and get even cooking and browning results. If you want to keep your food warm while you finish your work then use the warm function and set 6 hours. It is one of the best and economical ovens available in the market which consumes 50% less energy compare to other traditional ovens. It cooks your food faster but uses low heat to cook your

*Introduction*

food when you are using a convection setting. To reduce the mess the Oyster digital French door oven comes with a removable crumb tray. You can easily pull the tray for cleaning spills residues.

The Oster Digital French door oven cookbook contains 80 delicious and healthy recipes written from breakfast to desserts. All the recipes written in this cookbook are selected from globally inspired dishes and written into an easily understandable form. The recipes in this book are given with their perfect preparation and cooking time. Each and every recipe ends with their nutritional value information. This nutritional information will help you to keep track of daily intake of nutrients and calories. The book comes with a 30 days meal plan which helps you to plan your meal in advance. The advance meal plan saves your time and money. There are lots of cookbooks available in the market on this topic thanks for choosing this cookbook. I hope you love and enjoy the recipes written in this cookbook.

# BREAKFAST

# 1

## APPLE OAT CUPS

**Preparation Time:** 10 minutes
**Cooking Time:** 30 minutes
**Serve:** 12
**Ingredients:**
- 2 eggs
- 1 ¼ cups apples, peel & dice
- 2 tsp vanilla
- ½ cup applesauce
- 1 cup milk
- 2 tsp ground cinnamon
- 2 tsp baking powder
- 2 tbsp brown sugar
- 3 cups old-fashioned oats
- ¼ tsp salt

**Directions:**
1. Preheat the oven to 350 F.
2. Spray 12-cups muffin tin with cooking spray and set aside.
3. In a mixing bowl, mix oats, cinnamon, baking powder, brown sugar, and salt and set aside.
4. In large bowl, whisk eggs, vanilla, applesauce, and milk.

5. Add oat mixture into the egg mixture and stir until well combined.
6. Add apples and stir well.
7. Spoon mixture into the prepared muffin tin.
8. Place muffin tin onto the oven rack and bake for 30 minutes.
9. Serve and enjoy.

**Nutritional Value (Amount per Serving):**
- Calories 122
- Fat 2.5 g
- Carbohydrates 21.2 g
- Sugar 6.2 g
- Protein 4.3 g
- Cholesterol 29 mg

## 2

# SPINACH TOMATO EGG MUFFINS

**Preparation Time:** 10 minutes
**Cooking Time:** 20 minutes
**Serve:** 12
**Ingredients:**
- 8 eggs
- 1/3 cup feta cheese, crumbled
- ¼ cup almond milk
- 3 basil leaves, chopped
- ½ onion, diced
- 1 cup spinach, chopped
- ½ cup sun-dried tomatoes, chopped
- Pepper
- Salt

**Directions:**
1. Preheat the oven to 350 F.
2. Spray 12-cups muffin tin with cooking spray and set aside.
3. Divide feta cheese, basil, onion, spinach, and tomatoes evenly into the muffin tin cups.
4. In a bowl, whisk eggs with milk, pepper, and salt.
5. Pour egg mixture over veggies.

6. Place muffin tin onto the oven rack and bake for 18-20 minutes.

7. Serve and enjoy.

**Nutritional Value (Amount per Serving):**
- Calories 68
- Fat 5 g
- Carbohydrates 1.5 g
- Sugar 1 g
- Protein 4.6 g
- Cholesterol 113 mg

## 3

# PERFECT POTATO CASSEROLE

**Preparation Time:** 10 minutes
**Cooking Time:** 35 minutes
**Serve:** 10
**Ingredients:**
- 7 eggs
- 8 oz cheddar cheese, grated
- 20 oz frozen hash browns, diced
- ½ cup almond milk
- 1 onion, chopped & sautéed
- 1 lb sausage, cooked
- Pepper
- Salt

**Directions:**
1. Preheat the oven to 350 F.
2. Spray casserole dish with cooking spray and set aside.
3. In mixing bowl, whisk eggs with milk, pepper, and salt.
4. Add remaining ingredients and mix well. Pour egg mixture into the prepared casserole dish.
5. Place the casserole dish onto the oven rack and bake for 35 minutes.

6. Serve and enjoy.

**Nutritional Value (Amount per Serving):**
- Calories 393
- Fat 27.8 g
- Carbohydrates 18.5 g
- Sugar 1.7 g
- Protein 17 g
- Cholesterol 147 mg

# 4

## HAM CHEESE CASSEROLE

**Preparation Time:** 10 minutes
**Cooking Time:** 55 minutes
**Serve:** 12
**Ingredients:**
- 12 eggs
- 8 cups frozen hash browns
- 1 cup almond milk
- 8 oz cheddar cheese, shredded
- 16 oz ham, cubed
- ½ tsp pepper
- 1 tsp salt

**Directions:**
1. Preheat the oven to 350 F.
2. Spray a 9*13-inch baking dish with cooking spray and set aside.
3. In a bowl, mix cheese, ham, and frozen potatoes and pour into the prepared baking dish.
4. In a mixing bowl, whisk eggs with milk, pepper, and salt.
5. Pour egg mixture over cheese ham mixture.

6. Place baking dish onto the oven rack and bake for 55-60 minutes.

7. Serve and enjoy.

**Nutritional Value (Amount per Serving):**
- Calories 523
- Fat 31.7 g
- Carbohydrates 39.7 g
- Sugar 2.7 g
- Protein 20.1 g
- Cholesterol 205 mg

## 5

## FLUFFY BREAKFAST EGG MUFFINS

**Preparation Time:** 10 minutes
**Cooking Time:** 25 minutes
**Serve:** 12
**Ingredients:**
- 12 eggs
- 1/2 cup ham, diced
- 1/2 cup cheddar cheese, shredded
- 1/2 cup almond milk
- 1/4 tsp garlic powder
- Pepper
- Salt

**Directions:**
1. Preheat the oven to 375 F.
2. Spray 12-cups muffin tin with cooking spray and set aside.
3. In a bowl, whisk eggs with milk, garlic powder, pepper, and salt.
4. Add ham and cheese and stir well.
5. Pour egg mixture into the prepared muffin tin.
6. Place muffin tin onto the oven rack and bake for 25 minutes.
7. Serve and enjoy.

**Nutritional Value (Amount per Serving):**
- Calories 114
- Fat 8.8 g
- Carbohydrates 1.2 g
- Sugar 0.7 g
- Protein 7.9 g
- Cholesterol 172 mg

## 6

## PUMPKIN BREAD

**Preparation Time:** 10 minutes
**Cooking Time:** 35 minutes
**Serve:** 8
**Ingredients:**
- 2 eggs
- ¼ cup coconut flour
- ¼ cup flax seed meal
- ¼ cup Swerve
- 1 tsp baking powder
- 1 tsp pumpkin pie spice
- ¼ cup chocolate chips
- ½ cup pumpkin puree

**Directions:**
1. Preheat the oven to 350 F.
2. Grease loaf pan with and set aside.
3. Add all dry ingredients into the bowl and mix well. Set aside.
4. In a separate bowl, whisk pumpkin puree and eggs.
5. Pour wet ingredients mixture into the dry ingredients and mix until just combined.

6. Pour batter into the prepared loaf pan.
7. Place loaf pan onto the oven rack and bake for 35 minutes.
8. Slice and serve.

**Nutritional Value (Amount per Serving):**
- Calories 69
- Fat 3.8 g
- Carbohydrates 5.9 g
- Sugar 3.4 g
- Protein 2.6 g
- Cholesterol 42 mg

# 7

# HEALTHY BANANA BREAD

**Preparation Time:** 10 minutes
**Cooking Time:** 55 minutes
**Serve:** 12
**Ingredients:**
- 2 eggs
- 3 ripe bananas
- 1 tsp baking soda
- 1 cup sugar
- 1 tsp vanilla
- 1 stick butter, melted
- 2 cups flour
- 1/4 tsp ground cinnamon
- 1/2 tsp salt

**Directions:**
1. Preheat the oven to 350 F.
2. Add bananas and melted butter in a mixing bowl and mash with a fork.
3. Add eggs and vanilla and stir until well combined.
4. In a separate bowl, mix flour, baking soda, cinnamon, salt, and sugar.

5.Add flour mixture to the banana mixture and mix until just combined.

6.Pour batter into the greased 9*5-inch loaf pan.

7.Place loaf pan onto the oven rack and bake for 45-55 minutes.

8.Slice and serve.

**Nutritional Value (Amount per Serving):**
- Calories 244
- Fat 8.7 g
- Carbohydrates 39.5 g
- Sugar 20.5 g
- Protein 3.5 g
- Cholesterol 48 mg

## 8

# BAKED OATMEAL

**Preparation Time:** 10 minutes
**Cooking Time:** 20 minutes
**Serve:** 6
**Ingredients:**
- 1 egg
- 2 cups old fashioned oats
- 1 1/2 tsp baking powder
- 1/4 cup maple syrup
- 1 1/2 cups almond milk
- 1 cup strawberries, sliced
- 1 cup blueberries
- 1/2 tsp salt

**Directions:**
1. Preheat the oven to 375 F.
2. In a bowl, mix oats, salt, and baking powder.
3. Add egg, vanilla, maple syrup, and almond milk and stir well.
4. Add strawberries and blueberries and stir well.
5. Pour mixture into the greased baking dish.

6. Place a baking dish onto the oven rack and bake for 20 minutes.

7. Serve and enjoy.

**Nutritional Value (Amount per Serving):**
- Calories 413
- Fat 18.7 g
- Carbohydrates 53.9 g
- Sugar 14.9 g
- Protein 9.3 g
- Cholesterol 27 mg

## 9

# HEALTHY OAT MUFFINS

**Preparation Time:** 10 minutes
**Cooking Time:** 20 minutes
**Serve:** 12
**Ingredients:**
- 2 eggs
- 1 cup oats
- 1/2 cup plain yogurt
- 1/2 cup maple syrup
- 1 tbsp pumpkin pie spice
- 2 tsp baking powder
- 1 cup butternut squash puree
- 1 cup flour
- 1 tsp vanilla
- 1/3 cup olive oil
- 1/2 tsp sea salt

**Directions:**
1. Preheat the oven to 390 F.
2. Spray 12-cups muffin tray with cooking spray and set aside.
3. In a large bowl, whisk eggs with vanilla, oil, yogurt, butternut squash puree, and maple syrup.

4. In a separate bowl, mix flour, pumpkin pie spice, oats, oats, and salt.

5. Add flour mixture into the egg mixture and stir to combine.

6. Spoon the batter to the prepared muffin tray.

7. Place muffin tray onto the oven rack and bake for 20 minutes.

8. Serve and enjoy.

**Nutritional Value (Amount per Serving):**
- Calories 167
- Fat 7.1 g
- Carbohydrates 22.9 g
- Sugar 8.8 g
- Protein 3.5 g
- Cholesterol 28 mg

## 10

# BAKED CINNAMON OATMEAL

**Preparation Time:** 10 minutes
**Cooking Time:** 30 minutes
**Serve:** 8
**Ingredients:**
- 2 eggs
- 3 cups rolled oats
- 1 tsp ground cinnamon
- 1 tsp vanilla
- 1 1/2 tsp baking powder
- 1/4 cup butter, melted
- 1/2 cup maple syrup
- 1 1/2 cups almond milk
- Pinch of salt

**Directions:**
1. Preheat the oven to 350 F.
2. In a bowl, whisk eggs with almond milk, cinnamon, vanilla, baking powder, butter, maple syrup, and salt.
3. Add oats and mix well.
4. Pour mixture into the greased 8*8-inch baking pan.

5. Place the baking pan onto the oven rack and bake for 30 minutes.

6. Serve and enjoy.

**Nutritional Value (Amount per Serving):**
- Calories 341
- Fat 19.6 g
- Carbohydrates 37.3 g
- Sugar 13.7 g
- Protein 6.5 g
- Cholesterol 56 mg

# POULTRY

POETRY

## 11

# JUICY CHICKEN DRUMSTICKS

**Preparation Time:** 10 minutes
**Cooking Time:** 45 minutes
**Serve:** 6
**Ingredients:**
- 6 chicken legs
- ¼ cup soy sauce
- 2 tbsp olive oil
- ½ tsp paprika
- ½ tsp oregano
- 1 ½ tsp onion powder
- 1 tsp garlic powder
- ½ tsp pepper
- ½ tsp salt

**Directions:**
1. Preheat the oven to 375 F.
2. Add chicken legs and remaining ingredients into the zip-lock bag, seal bag shake well and place in the refrigerator for 1 hour.
3. Place rack onto a baking tray then arrange marinated chicken legs onto the rack. Insert into the oven.
4. Bake for 45 minutes.

5. Serve and enjoy.

**Nutritional Value (Amount per Serving):**
- Calories 315
- Fat 20.1 g
- Carbohydrates 1.9 g
- Sugar 0.5 g
- Protein 30.5 g
- Cholesterol 105 mg

## 12

# CRISPY CHICKEN WINGS

**Preparation Time:** 10 minutes
**Cooking Time:** 50 minutes
**Serve:** 6
**Ingredients:**
- 2 lbs chicken wings
- 1 tbsp baking powder
- 1 tsp Italian seasoning
- 1 tsp smoked paprika
- 1 tsp garlic powder
- 1/4 tsp pepper
- 1 tsp salt

**Directions:**
1. Preheat the oven to 425 F.
2. Add chicken wings and remaining ingredients into the mixing bowl and toss well.
3. Place rack onto a baking tray then arrange chicken wings onto the rack. Insert into the oven.
4. Bake for 30 minutes.
5. Turn chicken wings and bake for 20 minutes more.
6. Serve and enjoy.

**Nutritional Value (Amount per Serving):**
- Calories 295
- Fat 11.5 g
- Carbohydrates 1.9 g
- Sugar 0.2 g
- Protein 43.9 g
- Cholesterol 135 mg

## 13

# LEMON PEPPER CHICKEN WINGS

**Preparation Time:** 10 minutes
**Cooking Time:** 25 minutes
**Serve:** 6
**Ingredients:**
- 1 ½ lbs chicken wings
- 3 tbsp olive oil
- 2 tbsp honey
- ½ lemon juice
- ½ tsp pepper
- 6 tbsp butter, melted
- Pepper
- Salt

**Directions:**
1. Preheat the oven to 425 F.
2. Brush chicken wings with oil and season with pepper and salt.
3. Place rack onto a baking tray then arrange chicken wings onto the rack. Insert into the oven.
4. Bake for 25 minutes.
5. In a small bowl, mix honey, lemon juice, pepper, and butter.

6. Brush chicken wings with honey mixture and serve.

**Nutritional Value (Amount per Serving):**
- Calories 399
- Fat 26.9 g
- Carbohydrates 5.9 g
- Sugar 5.8 g
- Protein 33 g
- Cholesterol 131 mg

## 14

# DELICIOUS TURKEY CUTLETS

**Preparation Time:** 10 minutes
**Cooking Time:** 25 minutes
**Serve:** 4
**Ingredients:**
- 1 egg
- 1 ½ lbs turkey cutlets
- ½ tsp onion powder
- ¼ cup parmesan cheese, grated
- ½ cup breadcrumbs
- ½ tsp garlic powder
- ¼ tsp pepper
- ½ tsp salt

**Directions:**
1. Preheat the oven to 350 F.
2. Season turkey cutlets with pepper and salt.
3. In a small bowl, add egg and whisk well.
4. In a shallow dish, mix breadcrumbs, garlic powder, cheese, and onion powder.
5. Dip each cutlet in egg then coat with breadcrumb mixture.

6. Place coated cutlets onto the baking pan and bake in preheated oven for 25 minutes.

7. Serve and enjoy.

**Nutritional Value (Amount per Serving):**
- Calories 398
- Fat 12.6 g
- Carbohydrates 10.4 g
- Sugar 1.1 g
- Protein 56.1 g
- Cholesterol 177 mg

## 15

## TURKEY SPINACH PATTIES

**Preparation Time:** 10 minutes
**Cooking Time:** 30 minutes
**Serve:** 4
**Ingredients:**
- 1 lb ground turkey
- ¼ cup breadcrumbs
- 4 oz mozzarella cheese, cubed
- ¼ cup parsley, chopped
- ¼ cup basil, chopped
- 2 tbsp Worcestershire sauce
- 1 tsp lemon zest
- 2 tbsp vinegar
- ½ onion, diced
- 1 tsp garlic, minced
- 1 cup spinach, sautéed
- 1 tbsp olive oil
- Pepper
- Salt

**Directions:**
1. Preheat the oven to 350 F.

2.Add all ingredients into the large bowl and mix until well combined.

3.Make four equal shapes of patties from the mixture and place onto the baking pan.

4.Bake in preheated oven for 30-35 minutes.

5.Serve and enjoy.

**Nutritional Value (Amount per Serving):**
- Calories 407
- Fat 24.9 g
- Carbohydrates 9.6 g
- Sugar 2.6 g
- Protein 40.5 g
- Cholesterol 131 mg

## 16

# TURKEY MEATBALLS

**Preparation Time:** 10 minutes
**Cooking Time:** 20 minutes
**Serve:** 6
**Ingredients:**
- 1 egg
- 1 lb ground turkey
- 2 tsp onion powder
- 2 tbsp ketchup
- ¼ cup parmesan cheese, grated
- ½ cup breadcrumbs
- 1 tsp garlic powder
- 1 medium zucchini, grated
- 3 medium carrots, peeled & grated
- Pepper
- Salt

**Directions:**
1. Preheat the oven to 350 F.
2. Add all ingredients into the large bowl and mix until well combined.

3. Make equal shape of balls from mixture and place onto the parchment-lined baking sheet.
4. Bake in preheated oven for 20 minutes.
5. Serve and enjoy.

**Nutritional Value (Amount per Serving):**
- Calories 221
- Fat 9.6 g
- Carbohydrates 12.9 g
- Sugar 4.2 g
- Protein 23.7 g
- Cholesterol 104 mg

## 17

# HEALTHY CHICKEN FRITTERS

**Preparation Time:** 10 minutes
**Cooking Time:** 25 minutes
**Serve:** 4
**Ingredients:**
- 1 egg
- 1 lb ground chicken
- 1 ½ cups mozzarella cheese, shredded
- ¾ cup shallots, chopped
- 2 cups broccoli, cooked and chopped
- ¾ cup breadcrumbs
- 1 garlic clove, minced
- Pepper
- Salt

**Directions:**
1. Preheat the oven to 390 F.
2. Add all ingredients into the large bowl and mix until well combined.
3. Make small patties from the mixture and place onto the parchment-lined baking sheet.
4. Bake for 15 minutes. Flip and bake for 10 minutes more.

5. Serve and enjoy.

**Nutritional Value (Amount per Serving):**
- Calories 379
- Fat 12.6 g
- Carbohydrates 23.4 g
- Sugar 2.1 g
- Protein 42 g
- Cholesterol 147 mg

## 18

# CREAMY CHICKEN

**Preparation Time:** 10 minutes
**Cooking Time:** 55 minutes
**Serve:** 4
**Ingredients:**
- 4 chicken breasts
- 1 tsp garlic powder
- 1 tsp dried basil
- 1 tsp dried oregano
- ¾ cup parmesan cheese, grated
- 1 cup sour cream
- 1 cup mozzarella cheese, shredded
- Pepper
- Salt

**Directions:**
1. Preheat the oven to 375 F.
2. Spray casserole dish with cooking spray and set aside.
3. Place chicken breasts into the prepared casserole dish and top with mozzarella cheese.
4. In a bowl, mix sour cream, parmesan cheese, oregano, basil, garlic powder, pepper, and salt.

5. Pour sour cream mixture over chicken breasts.

6. Place casserole dish onto the oven rack and bake for 55-60 minutes.

7. Serve and enjoy.

**Nutritional Value (Amount per Serving):**
- Calories 574
- Fat 33.2 g
- Carbohydrates 3.5 g
- Sugar 0.3 g
- Protein 58.3 g
- Cholesterol 189 mg

## 19

# EASY BROWN SUGAR CHICKEN

**Preparation Time:** 10 minutes
**Cooking Time:** 30 minutes
**Serve:** 4
**Ingredients:**
- 4 chicken breasts, boneless & skinless
- ¼ cup brown sugar
- 1 tbsp garlic, minced & sautéed
- Pepper
- Salt

**Directions:**
1. Preheat the oven to 450 F.
2. Spray casserole dish with cooking spray and set aside.
3. Season chicken breasts with pepper and salt and place into the casserole dish.
4. Mix together brown sugar and garlic and sprinkle over chicken.
5. Place casserole dish onto the oven rack and bake for 25-30 minutes.
6. Serve and enjoy.

**Nutritional Value (Amount per Serving):**

- Calories 345
- Fat 14.3 g
- Carbohydrates 9.6 g
- Sugar 8.8 g
- Protein 42.4 g
- Cholesterol 130 mg

## 20

## CHICKEN MEATBALLS

**Preparation Time:** 10 minutes
**Cooking Time:** 25 minutes
**Serve:** 6
**Ingredients:**
- 1 egg
- 1 lb ground chicken
- ¼ cup fresh parsley, chopped
- ½ tsp dried oregano
- ½ tsp garlic powder
- ½ cup parmesan cheese, grated
- ½ cup breadcrumbs
- ½ tsp onion powder
- 1 tsp pepper
- ½ tsp salt

**Directions:**
1. Preheat the oven to 400 F.
2. Add all ingredients into the mixing bowl and mix until well combined.
3. Make equal shape of balls from meat mixture and place onto the parchment-lined baking sheet.

4. Bake in preheated oven for 25-30 minutes.
5. Serve and enjoy.

**Nutritional Value (Amount per Serving):**
- Calories 193
- Fat 6.9 g
- Carbohydrates 7.3 g
- Sugar 0.8 g
- Protein 24.2 g
- Cholesterol 95 mg

# BEEF, PORK & LAMB

## 21

# BEEF ONION BAKE

**Preparation Time:** 10 minutes
**Cooking Time:** 30 minutes
**Serve:** 6
**Ingredients:**
- 1 lb ground beef
- 2 cups fried onions
- 2 cups cheddar cheese, shredded
- 1 tsp Worcestershire sauce
- 1 tsp garlic powder
- 16 oz French onion dip
- 10.5 oz cream of mushrooms soup
- 10 oz pasta, uncooked

**Directions:**
1. Preheat the oven to 350 F.
2. Cook pasta according to the packet instructions and drain well.
3. Brown the meat with Worcestershire sauce and garlic powder over medium heat. Drain meat.
4. Add onion dip and cream of mushroom soup into the browned meat and simmer for 5 minutes over low heat.

5. Add pasta to the meat mixture and mix well. Pour meat mixture into the greased 9*13-inch casserole dish and top with cheddar cheese and fried onions.

6. Place casserole dish onto the oven rack and bake for 20-25 minutes.

7. Serve and enjoy.

**Nutritional Value (Amount per Serving):**
- Calories 742
- Fat 44.5 g
- Carbohydrates 43 g
- Sugar 3.3 g
- Protein 40.9 g
- Cholesterol 193 mg

## 22

# SIMPLE SPICED PORK CHOPS

**Preparation Time:** 10 minutes
**Cooking Time:** 20 minutes
**Serve:** 4
**Ingredients:**
- 4 pork chops, boneless
- 2 tbsp olive oil
- For the dry rub:
- 1/4 tsp pepper
- 1/2 tsp Italian seasoning
- 1/2 tsp garlic powder
- 2 tbsp brown sugar
- 1 tsp smoked paprika
- 1/2 tsp sea salt

**Directions:**
1. Preheat the oven to 375 F.
2. Brush pork chops with olive oil.
3. In a small bowl, mix together all rub ingredients and rub all over pork chops.
4. Place pork chops onto the baking pan and bake in preheated oven for 20-25 minutes.

5. Serve and enjoy.

**Nutritional Value (Amount per Serving):**
- Calories 338
- Fat 27.1 g
- Carbohydrates 5.1 g
- Sugar 4.6 g
- Protein 18.1 g
- Cholesterol 69 mg

## 23

# QUICK RANCH PORK CHOPS

**Preparation Time:** 10 minutes
**Cooking Time:** 30 minutes
**Serve:** 6
**Ingredients:**
- 6 pork chops, boneless
- 1 tsp dried parsley
- 2 tbsp dry ranch mix
- 4 tbsp olive oil

**Directions:**
1. Preheat the oven to 425 F.
2. Place pork chops into the baking dish.
3. Mix oil, dry ranch mix, and parsley and spoon over pork chops.
4. Place baking dish onto the oven rack and bake for 30 minutes.
5. Serve and enjoy.

**Nutritional Value (Amount per Serving):**
- Calories 336
- Fat 29.2 g

- Carbohydrates 0 g
- Sugar 0 g
- Protein 18 g
- Cholesterol 69 mg

## 24

# PORK CHOPS WITH POTATOES

**Preparation Time:** 10 minutes
**Cooking Time:** 20 minutes
**Serve:** 6
**Ingredients:**
- 6 pork chops, bone-in
- 1 oz dried Italian dressing mix
- ¼ cup olive oil
- 1 onion, chopped
- 1 lb baby potatoes, quartered
- Pepper
- Salt

**Directions:**
1. Preheat the oven to 425 F.
2. Arrange pork chops, onions, and potatoes onto the greased baking pan.
3. In a small bowl, mix oil, Italian dressing mix, pepper, and salt, and spoon over pork chops.
4. Place the baking pan onto the oven rack and bake for 15-20 minutes.
5. Serve and enjoy.

**Nutritional Value (Amount per Serving):**
- Calories 393
- Fat 28.5 g
- Carbohydrates 14.1 g
- Sugar 0.8 g
- Protein 20.3 g
- Cholesterol 69 mg

## 25
## BAKED PORK PATTIES

**Preparation Time:** 10 minutes
**Cooking Time:** 30 minutes
**Serve:** 6
**Ingredients:**
- 1 egg
- 2 ¼ lbs ground pork
- ½ cup breadcrumbs
- 1 tsp garlic powder
- 1 tsp paprika
- 1 onion, minced
- 1 carrot, minced
- ½ tsp pepper
- 1 tsp salt

**Directions:**
1. Preheat the oven to 375 F.
2. Add all ingredients into the mixing bowl and mix until well combined.
3. Make six equal shapes of patties from mixture and place onto the greased baking pan and bake in preheated oven for 25-35 minutes.

4. Serve and enjoy.

**Nutritional Value (Amount per Serving):**
- Calories 304
- Fat 7.3 g
- Carbohydrates 9.9 g
- Sugar 2.1 g
- Protein 47.1 g
- Cholesterol 151 mg

## 26

# MEATBALLS

**Preparation Time:** 10 minutes
**Cooking Time:** 20 minutes
**Serve:** 4
**Ingredients:**
- 1 lb ground lamb
- ¼ tsp dried basil
- ¼ tsp dried oregano
- 1 garlic clove, minced
- ¼ cup fresh cilantro, chopped
- ¼ cup raisins
- ¼ cup yogurt
- 2 bread slices, cut into small pieces
- Pepper
- Salt

**Directions:**
1. Preheat the oven to 375 F.
2. Add all ingredients into the mixing bowl and mix until well combined.
3. Make equal shape of balls from meat mixture and place onto the parchment-lined baking pan.

4. Bake for 20 minutes.
5. Serve and enjoy.

**Nutritional Value (Amount per Serving):**
- Calories 263
- Fat 8.7 g
- Carbohydrates 10.9 g
- Sugar 6.7 g
- Protein 33.4 g
- Cholesterol 103 mg

## 27

# SIMPLE LAMB PATTIES

**Preparation Time:** 10 minutes
**Cooking Time:** 20 minutes
**Serve:** 6
**Ingredients:**
- 1 ½ lbs ground lamb
- 1 tbsp fresh ginger, grated
- 3 green onions, sliced
- Pepper
- Salt

**Directions:**
1. Preheat the oven to 375 F.
2. Add all ingredients into the mixing bowl and mix until well combined.
3. Make six equal shapes of patties from meat mixture and place onto the parchment-lined baking pan.
4. Bake for 20 minutes.
5. Serve and enjoy.

**Nutritional Value (Amount per Serving):**
- Calories 216

- Fat 8.4 g
- Carbohydrates 1.2 g
- Sugar 0.2 g
- Protein 32.1 g
- Cholesterol 102 mg

## 28

## BAKED PORK RIBS

**Preparation Time:** 10 minutes
**Cooking Time:** 30 minutes
**Serve:** 8
**Ingredients:**
- 2 lbs pork ribs, boneless
- 1 tbsp onion powder
- 1 ½ tbsp garlic powder
- ½ tsp Italian seasoning
- 2 tbsp olive oil
- Pepper
- Salt

**Directions:**
1. Preheat the oven to 350 F.
2. In a small bowl, mix onion powder, garlic powder, Italian seasoning, pepper, and salt.
3. Brush pork ribs with oil and rub with spices mixture.
4. Place pork ribs onto the baking pan and bake for 25-30 minutes.
5. Serve and enjoy.

**Nutritional Value (Amount per Serving):**

- Calories 319
- Fat 20.2 g
- Carbohydrates 1.9 g
- Sugar 0.7 g
- Protein 30.4 g
- Cholesterol 117 mg

## 29

# JUICY PORK TENDERLOIN

**Preparation Time:** 10 minutes
**Cooking Time:** 20 minutes
**Serve:** 6
**Ingredients:**
- 2 lbs pork tenderloin
- ¼ cup honey
- ¼ cup soy sauce
- 1 tbsp garlic, minced
- 1 tsp dried oregano
- 1 tbsp olive oil
- Pepper
- Salt

**Directions:**
1. Preheat the oven to 350 F.
2. Add honey and soy sauce into the small saucepan and cook until reduced by half.
3. Mix garlic, oregano, pepper, and salt and rub all over pork tenderloin.
4. Heat oil in a large pan over medium heat. Cook tenderloin on each side for 2 minutes.

5. Place pork tenderloin onto the baking sheet and baste with honey mixture.
6. Bake in preheated oven for 20 minutes.
7. Slice and serve.

**Nutritional Value (Amount per Serving):**
- Calories 288
- Fat 7.7 g
- Carbohydrates 13.1 g
- Sugar 11.8 g
- Protein 40.4 g
- Cholesterol 110 mg

## 30

# ROSEMARY PORK CHOPS

**Preparation Time:** 10 minutes
**Cooking Time:** 25 minutes
**Serve:** 4
**Ingredients:**
- 4 pork chops, boneless and cut 1/2-inch thick
- 1 tsp dried rosemary, crushed
- 1 tbsp olive oil
- 1/4 tsp pepper
- 1/4 tsp salt

**Directions:**
1. Preheat the oven to 350 F.
2. Season pork chops with pepper and salt.
3. Mix rosemary and oil and rub all over pork chops.
4. Place pork chops onto the baking pan and bake for 25 minutes.
5. Serve and enjoy.

**Nutritional Value (Amount per Serving):**
- Calories 257
- Fat 19.9 g

- Carbohydrates 0.3 g
- Sugar 0 g
- Protein 18 g
- Cholesterol 69 mg

## 31

# GREEK LAMB PATTIES

**Preparation Time:** 10 minutes
**Cooking Time:** 8 minutes
**Serve:** 4
**Ingredients:**
- 1 lb ground lamb
- 1 cup feta cheese, crumbled
- 1 tbsp garlic, minced
- 1 jalapeno pepper, minced
- 4 basil leaves, minced
- 10 mint leaves, minced
- 1/4 cup fresh parsley, chopped
- 1 tsp dried oregano
- 1/4 tsp pepper
- 1/2 tsp kosher salt

**Directions:**
1. Preheat the oven to 390 F.
2. All ingredients into the mixing bowl and mix until well combined.
3. Make four equal shapes of patties and place them onto the baking pan.

4. Bake for 8 minutes.
5. Serve and enjoy.

**Nutritional Value (Amount per Serving):**
- Calories 317
- Fat 16.4 g
- Carbohydrates 3 g
- Sugar 1.7 g
- Protein 37.5 g
- Cholesterol 135 mg

## 32

# LAMB MEATBALLS

**Preparation Time:** 10 minutes
**Cooking Time:** 20 minutes
**Serve:** 4
**Ingredients:**
- 1 egg, lightly beaten
- 1 lb ground lamb
- 2 tsp fresh oregano, chopped
- 2 tbsp fresh parsley, chopped
- 1 tbsp garlic, minced
- 1/4 tsp pepper
- 1/4 tsp red pepper flakes
- 1 tsp ground cumin
- 1 tsp kosher salt

**Directions:**
1. Preheat the oven to 425 F.
2. Add all ingredients into the mixing bowl and mix until well combined.
3. Make small balls from the meat mixture and place onto baking sheet.
4. Bake for 20 minutes.

5. Serve and enjoy.

**Nutritional Value (Amount per Serving):**
- Calories 325
- Fat 20.2 g
- Carbohydrates 1.7 g
- Sugar 0.2 g
- Protein 33.6 g
- Cholesterol 143 mg

## 33

# PORK MEATBALLS

**Preparation Time:** 10 minutes
**Cooking Time:** 15 minutes
**Serve:** 4
**Ingredients:**
- 1 lb ground pork
- 1 tsp smoked paprika
- 1 tsp garlic powder
- 1 tsp onion powder
- 1/2 tsp ground cumin
- 1/2 tsp coriander
- 1/2 tsp dried thyme
- Pepper
- Salt

**Directions:**
1. Preheat the oven to 400 F.
2. Add all ingredients into the large bowl and mix until well combined.
3. Make small balls from the meat mixture and place onto the baking sheet.
4. Bake for 15 minutes.

5. Serve and enjoy.

**Nutritional Value (Amount per Serving):**
- Calories 170
- Fat 4.1 g
- Carbohydrates 1.5 g
- Sugar 0.4 g
- Protein 30 g
- Cholesterol 83 mg

## 34

# BEEF ZUCCHINI BURGER PATTIES

**Preparation Time:** 10 minutes
**Cooking Time:** 35 minutes
**Serve:** 6
**Ingredients:**
- 1 lb ground beef
- 2 eggs, lightly beaten
- 1/2 onion, chopped
- 2 medium zucchini, grated and squeeze out all liquid
- 1/2 tsp chili powder
- 1 tsp curry powder
- 1 cup breadcrumbs
- Pepper
- Salt

**Directions:**
1. Preheat the oven to 400 F.
2. Add all ingredients into the large bowl and mix until well combined.
3. Make six equal shapes patties from meat mixture and place onto baking sheet.
4. Bake for 35 minutes.

5. Serve and enjoy.

**Nutritional Value (Amount per Serving):**
- Calories 248
- Fat 7.3 g
- Carbohydrates 16.4 g
- Sugar 2.8 g
- Protein 28.1 g
- Cholesterol 122 mg

## 35

# SMOKED PAPRIKA PORK CHOPS

**Preparation Time:** 10 minutes
**Cooking Time:** 25 minutes
**Serve:** 2
**Ingredients:**
- 2 pork chops
- 2 tsp brown sugar
- 1 tsp smoked paprika
- Pepper
- Salt

**Directions:**
1. Preheat the oven to 325 F.
2. Mix smoked paprika, brown sugar, pepper, and salt and rub all over pork chops.
3. Place pork chops into the baking dish.
4. Bake for 25 minutes.
5. Serve and enjoy.

**Nutritional Value (Amount per Serving):**
- Calories 271
- Fat 20 g

- Carbohydrates 3.6 g
- Sugar 3 g
- Protein 18.1 g
- Cholesterol 69 mg

# FISH & SEAFOOD

## 36

## BAKED SALMON PATTIES

**Preparation Time:** 10 minutes
**Cooking Time:** 20 minutes
**Serve:** 4
**Ingredients:**
- 2 eggs, lightly beaten
- 14 oz can salmon, drained and flaked with a fork
- 1/4 cup breadcrumbs
- 1 tbsp garlic, minced
- 1/2 cup fresh parsley, chopped
- 1 tsp Dijon mustard
- Pepper
- Salt

**Directions:**
1. Preheat the oven to 400 F.
2. Add all ingredients into the large bowl and mix until well combined.
3. Make four equal shapes of patties from the mixture and place onto the baking sheet.
4. Bake for 10 minutes.
5. Flip patties and bake for 10 minutes more.

6. Serve and enjoy.

**Nutritional Value (Amount per Serving):**
- Calories 203
- Fat 8.7 g
- Carbohydrates 6.3 g
- Sugar 0.7 g
- Protein 23.7 g
- Cholesterol 136 mg

## 37

## SIMPLE CAJUN SALMON

**Preparation Time:** 10 minutes
**Cooking Time:** 12 minutes
**Serve:** 4
**Ingredients:**
- 4 salmon fillets
- 1 ½ tsp Cajun seasoning
- ¼ cup brown sugar
- Pepper
- Salt

**Directions:**
1. Preheat the oven to 400 F.
2. Mix brown sugar, Cajun seasoning, pepper, and salt and rub all over salmon fillets.
3. Place salmon fillets onto the baking pan and bake for 12 minutes.
4. Serve and enjoy.

**Nutritional Value (Amount per Serving):**
- Calories 270
- Fat 10 g

- Carbohydrates 8 g
- Sugar 8 g
- Protein 34 g
- Cholesterol 75 mg

## 38

## TASTY CRAB PATTIES

**Preparation Time:** 10 minutes
**Cooking Time:** 30 minutes
**Serve:** 6
**Ingredients:**
- 15 oz lump crab meat
- 1/4 cup celery, diced
- 1/4 cup onion, diced
- 1 cup crushed crackers
- 1 tsp old bay seasoning
- 1 tsp mustard
- 2/3 cup mashed avocado

**Directions:**
1. Preheat the oven to 350 F.
2. Add all ingredients into the mixing bowl and mix until just combined.
3. Make six equal shapes of patties from the mixture and place onto the baking sheet.
4. Bake for 30 minutes.
5. Serve and enjoy.

**Nutritional Value (Amount per Serving):**

- Calories 155
- Fat 12 g
- Carbohydrates 12 g
- Sugar 2 g
- Protein 12 g
- Cholesterol 42 mg

## 39

# GARLIC BUTTER SHRIMP

**Preparation Time:** 10 minutes
**Cooking Time:** 15 minutes
**Serve:** 4
**Ingredients:**
- 1 lb shrimp, peel & deveined
- 4 garlic cloves, pressed
- 2 tbsp butter, melted
- 2 tbsp fresh lemon juice

**Directions:**
1. Preheat the oven to 375 F.
2. Add shrimp, garlic, butter, and lemon juice into the mixing bowl and toss well.
3. Pour shrimp into the baking pan.
4. Place the baking pan onto the oven rack and bake for 15 minutes.
5. Serve and enjoy.

**Nutritional Value (Amount per Serving):**
- Calories 196
- Fat 7.5 g

- Carbohydrates 4.5 g
- Sugar 0.5 g
- Protein 25.1 g
- Cholesterol 255 mg

## 40

# SWEET DIJON SALMON

**Preparation Time:** 10 minutes
**Cooking Time:** 12 minutes
**Serve:** 4
**Ingredients:**
- 4 salmon fillets
- 2 tbsp olive oil
- 1 tsp garlic, minced
- 4 tbsp maple syrup
- ¼ cup Dijon mustard

**Directions:**
1. Preheat the oven to 400 F.
2. In a small bowl, mix oil, garlic, maple syrup, and Dijon mustard.
3. Brush salmon fillets with oil mixture and place onto the baking pan.
4. Bake for 12 minutes.
5. Serve and enjoy.

**Nutritional Value (Amount per Serving):**
- Calories 361

- Fat 18 g
- Carbohydrates 15 g
- Sugar 12 g
- Protein 34 g
- Cholesterol 75 mg

## 41

# FLAVORFUL SHRIMP FAJITAS

**Preparation Time:** 10 minutes
**Cooking Time:** 15 minutes
**Serve:** 4
**Ingredients:**
- 1 lb shrimp, peeled & deveined
- 2 tbsp olive oil
- 1 tbsp taco seasoning
- ½ lemon juice
- 1 onion, sliced
- 1 red bell pepper, sliced
- 2 yellow bell pepper, sliced

**Directions:**
1. Preheat the oven to 400 F.
2. Add shrimp and remaining ingredients into the mixing bowl and mix well.
3. Pour shrimp mixture into the baking pan.
4. Place the baking pan onto the oven rack and bake for 15 minutes.
5. Serve and enjoy.

**Nutritional Value (Amount per Serving):**

- Calories 230
- Fat 8 g
- Carbohydrates 12 g
- Sugar 5 g
- Protein 25 g
- Cholesterol 240 mg

## 42

## DELICIOUS PESTO SALMON

**Preparation Time:** 10 minutes
**Cooking Time:** 20 minutes
**Serve:** 4
**Ingredients:**
- 4 salmon fillets
- 1 onion, sliced
- 2 cups cherry tomatoes, cut in half
- ½ cup feta cheese, crumbled
- ½ cup basil pesto
- Pepper
- Salt

**Directions:**
1. Preheat the oven to 350 F.
2. Season salmon fillets with pepper and salt and place into the baking dish.
3. Pour remaining ingredients over salmon fillets.
4. Bake for 20 minutes.
5. Serve and enjoy.

**Nutritional Value (Amount per Serving):**
- Calories 445

- Fat 28 g
- Carbohydrates 8 g
- Sugar 6 g
- Protein 40 g
- Cholesterol 102 mg

## 43

# GARLIC TILAPIA

**Preparation Time:** 10 minutes
**Cooking Time:** 15 minutes
**Serve:** 4
**Ingredients:**
- 1 lb tilapia fillets
- 2 tbsp olive oil
- 5 garlic cloves, minced
- Pepper
- Salt

**Directions:**
1. Preheat the oven to 400 F.
2. Season fish fillets with pepper and salt and place into the baking dish.
3. Mix oil and garlic and pour over fish fillets.
4. Place a baking dish onto the oven rack and bake for 15 minutes.
5. Serve and enjoy.

**Nutritional Value (Amount per Serving):**
- Calories 161

- Fat 8 g
- Carbohydrates 1 g
- Sugar 0.1 g
- Protein 20 g
- Cholesterol 55 mg

## 44

# FLAVORS CATFISH FILLETS

**Preparation Time:** 10 minutes
**Cooking Time:** 15 minutes
**Serve:** 4
**Ingredients:**
- 1 lb catfish fillets
- 1 tbsp dried oregano, crushed
- 1 ½ tsp onion powder
- 1 tsp red chili flakes
- ½ tsp chili powder
- ½ tsp ground cumin
- Pepper
- Salt

**Directions:**
1. Preheat the oven to 350 F.
2. In a small bowl, mix cumin, chili powder, red chili flakes, onion powder, oregano, pepper, and salt and rub over fish fillets.
3. Place fish fillets into the baking dish.
4. Place a baking dish onto the oven rack and bake for 15 minutes.
5. Serve and enjoy.

**Nutritional Value (Amount per Serving):**
- Calories 166
- Fat 9 g
- Carbohydrates 2 g
- Sugar 0.5 g
- Protein 19 g
- Cholesterol 55 mg

## 45

## BLACKENED FISH FILLETS

**Preparation Time:** 10 minutes
**Cooking Time:** 12 minutes
**Serve:** 4
**Ingredients:**
- 4 mahi-mahi fillets
- ½ tsp onion powder
- 1 tsp ground cumin
- 1 tsp dried oregano
- ½ tsp cayenne
- 3 tbsp olive oil
- 1 tsp garlic powder
- 1 tsp smoked paprika
- ½ tsp pepper
- ½ tsp salt

**Directions:**
1. Preheat the oven to 400 F.
2. In a small bowl, mix onion powder, cumin, oregano, cayenne, garlic powder, paprika, pepper, and salt.
3. Brush fish fillets with oil and rub with spice mixture.
4. Place fish fillets into the baking dish.

5. Place baking dish onto the oven rack and bake for 12 minutes.

6. Serve and enjoy.

**Nutritional Value (Amount per Serving):**
- Calories 190
- Fat 12 g
- Carbohydrates 2 g
- Sugar 0.5 g
- Protein 20 g
- Cholesterol 85 mg

# VEGETABLES & SIDE DISHES

## 46

# PARMESAN CAULIFLOWER FLORETS

**Preparation Time:** 10 minutes
**Cooking Time:** 30 minutes
**Serve:** 6
**Ingredients:**
- 1 medium cauliflower head, cut into florets
- ½ cup parmesan cheese, grated
- 1 cup breadcrumbs
- 1 tsp garlic, minced
- ½ cup butter, melted
- ¼ tsp pepper
- ¼ tsp salt

**Directions:**
1. Preheat the oven to 400 F.
2. In a small bowl, mix melted butter and garlic.
3. In a shallow dish, mix parmesan cheese, breadcrumbs, pepper, and salt.
4. Dip each cauliflower floret into the melted butter and coat with parmesan cheese mixture and place onto the parchment-lined baking pan.
5. Bake in preheated oven for 30 minutes.

6. Serve and enjoy.

**Nutritional Value (Amount per Serving):**
- Calories 280
- Fat 19.6 g
- Carbohydrates 18.3 g
- Sugar 3.4 g
- Protein 9.8 g
- Cholesterol 51 mg

## 47

# ZUCCHINI TOMATO BAKE

**Preparation Time:** 10 minutes
**Cooking Time:** 30 minutes
**Serve:** 6
**Ingredients:**
- 2 medium zucchini, sliced
- 5 medium tomatoes, sliced
- 2 medium yellow squash, sliced
- ½ tsp Italian seasoning
- ½ tsp onion powder
- ½ tsp garlic powder
- ½ cup parmesan cheese, shredded
- ½ tsp pepper

**Directions:**
1. Preheat the oven to 375 F.
2. In a greased baking dish, arrange zucchini, tomatoes, and squash in an alternating pattern.
3. Top with spices and cheese.
4. Bake for 25-30 minutes.
5. Serve and enjoy.

**Nutritional Value (Amount per Serving):**

- Calories 60
- Fat 2.3 g
- Carbohydrates 7 g
- Sugar 4 g
- Protein 4.4 g
- Cholesterol 5 mg

## 48

# ZUCCHINI POTATO GRATIN

**Preparation Time:** 10 minutes
**Cooking Time:** 50 minutes
**Serve:** 6
**Ingredients:**
- 1 ½ zucchini, cut into ¼-inch slices
- 5 small potatoes, cut into 1/8-inch slices
- 1 cup Gruyere cheese, grated
- 1 cup half and half
- 1 tsp herb de Provence
- 1 tsp garlic, minced
- ¼ tsp pepper
- 1 ¾ tsp salt

**Directions:**
1. Preheat the oven to 400 F.
2. Arrange vegetables in a circular pattern in a greased 8*6-inch baking dish
3. Mix half and half, herb de Provence, garlic, pepper, and salt and pour over vegetables.
4. Sprinkle grated cheese on top.
5. Bake for 50 minutes.

6. Serve and enjoy.

**Nutritional Value (Amount per Serving):**
- Calories 256
- Fat 6 g
- Carbohydrates 31 g
- Sugar 2 g
- Protein 10 g
- Cholesterol 35 mg

## 49

# SPINACH ZUCCHINI CASSEROLE

**Preparation Time:** 10 minutes
**Cooking Time:** 40 minutes
**Serve:** 6
**Ingredients:**
- 2 egg whites
- 3 cups baby spinach
- 2 small zucchini, diced
- ¼ cup parmesan cheese, grated
- 2 tsp garlic powder
- 1 tsp dried basil
- ½ cup breadcrumbs
- 2 small yellow squash, diced
- ¼ cup feta cheese, crumbled
- 1 tbsp olive oil
- ½ tsp pepper
- ½ tsp kosher salt

**Directions:**
1. Preheat the oven to 400 F.
2. Spray 9*13-inch casserole dish with cooking spray and set aside.

3. Heat oil in a pan over medium heat. Add squash, spinach, and zucchini into the pan and sauté for 5 minutes. Drain excess liquid and transfer vegetables into the mixing bowl.

4. Add remaining ingredients into the mixing bowl and mix well.

5. Pour mixture into the prepared casserole dish.

6. Place the casserole dish onto the oven rack and bake for 40 minutes.

7. Serve and enjoy.

**Nutritional Value (Amount per Serving):**
- Calories 102
- Fat 3.6 g
- Carbohydrates 10.8 g
- Sugar 2.6 g
- Protein 6.9 g
- Cholesterol 11 mg

## 50

# HEALTHY CARROT FRIES

**Preparation Time:** 10 minutes
**Cooking Time:** 25 minutes
**Serve:** 4
**Ingredients:**
- 4 medium carrots, peel & cut into fries shape
- 1 tsp ground cumin
- ½ tbsp smoked paprika
- 1 ½ tbsp olive oil
- ½ tsp salt

**Directions:**
1. Preheat the oven to 450 F.
2. Toss carrot fries with cumin, paprika, oil, and salt.
3. Arrange carrot fries onto the baking sheet and bake for 15 minutes.
4. Flip fries and bake for 10 minutes more.
5. Serve and enjoy.

**Nutritional Value (Amount per Serving):**
- Calories 85
- Fat 6 g

- Carbohydrates 7 g
- Sugar 3 g
- Protein 1 g
- Cholesterol 0 mg

## 51

## BAKED CURRIED CAULIFLOWER FLORETS

**Preparation Time:** 10 minutes
**Cooking Time:** 15 minutes
**Serve:** 4
**Ingredients:**
- 2 lbs cauliflower, cut into florets
- 2 tsp fresh lemon juice
- 1 1/2 tsp curry powder
- 1 tbsp olive oil
- 1 tsp kosher salt

**Directions:**
1. Preheat the oven to 425 F.
2. Toss cauliflower florets with curry powder, oil, and salt.
3. Spread cauliflower florets onto the baking sheet and bake for 15 minutes.
4. Drizzle with lemon juice and serve.

**Nutritional Value (Amount per Serving):**
- Calories 90
- Fat 4 g
- Carbohydrates 12 g

PAMELA KENDRICK

- Sugar 5 g
- Protein 4 g
- Cholesterol 0 mg

## 52

# BALSAMIC MUSHROOMS

**Preparation Time:** 10 minutes
**Cooking Time:** 20 minutes
**Serve:** 6
**Ingredients:**
- 1 lb button mushrooms, scrubbed
- 1/2 tsp dried oregano
- 1 tbsp garlic, crushed
- 2 tbsp olive oil
- 4 tbsp balsamic vinegar
- 1/2 tsp dried basil
- 1/4 tsp black pepper
- 1 tsp sca salt

**Directions:**
1. Preheat the oven to 425 F.
2. In a mixing bowl, add mushrooms and remaining ingredients and mix well and let it sit for 15 minutes.
3. Spread mushrooms onto the baking sheet and bake for 20 minutes.
4. Serve and enjoy.

**Nutritional Value (Amount per Serving):**

- Calories 60
- Fat 5 g
- Carbohydrates 3 g
- Sugar 1.5 g
- Protein 2.5 g
- Cholesterol 0 mg

## 53

# CHEESY BROCCOLI FRITTERS

**Preparation Time:** 10 minutes
**Cooking Time:** 30 minutes
**Serve:** 4
**Ingredients:**
- 3 cups broccoli florets, cooked & chopped
- 2 garlic cloves, minced
- 2 eggs, lightly beaten
- ¼ cup breadcrumbs
- 2 cups cheddar cheese, shredded
- Pepper
- Salt

**Directions:**
1. Preheat the oven to 375 F.
2. Add all ingredients into the large bowl and mix until well combined.
3. Make equal shapes of patties from mixture and place onto the parchment-lined baking sheet and bake for 30 minutes. Flip patties halfway through.
4. Serve and enjoy.

**Nutritional Value (Amount per Serving):**

- Calories 295
- Fat 20 g
- Carbohydrates 6 g
- Sugar 1.7 g
- Protein 19.2 g
- Cholesterol 141 mg

## 54

# CREAMY BROCCOLI CASSEROLE

**Preparation Time:** 10 minutes
**Cooking Time:** 30 minutes
**Serve:** 6
**Ingredients:**
- 15 oz frozen broccoli florets, defrosted and drained
- 1/3 cup milk
- 1/2 tsp onion powder
- 10.5 oz can cream of mushroom soup
- 1 cup cheddar cheese, shredded
- For topping:
- 1 tbsp butter, melted
- 1/2 cup cracker crumbs

**Directions:**
1. Preheat the oven to 350 F.
2. Add all ingredients except topping ingredients into the greased casserole dish.
3. In a small bowl, mix cracker crumbs and butter and sprinkle over dish mixture.
4. Place the casserole dish onto the oven rack and bake for 30 minutes.

5. Serve and enjoy.

**Nutritional Value (Amount per Serving):**
- Calories 192
- Fat 12.9 g
- Carbohydrates 10.5 g
- Sugar 2.4 g
- Protein 6.9 g
- Cholesterol 25 mg

## 55

## BAKED SWEET POTATOES & APPLE

**Preparation Time:** 10 minutes
**Cooking Time:** 30 minutes
**Serve:** 2
**Ingredients:**
- 2 large green apples, diced
- 2 large sweet potatoes, diced
- 2 tbsp maple syrup
- 1 tbsp olive oil
- 2 tsp cinnamon

**Directions:**
1. Preheat the oven to 400 F.
2. In a mixing bowl, toss sweet potatoes, apples, cinnamon, and oil.
3. Spread sweet potatoes and apples onto the baking pan and bake in a preheated oven for 30 minutes.
4. Drizzle with maple syrup and serve.

**Nutritional Value (Amount per Serving):**
- Calories 350
- Fat 7 g

- Carbohydrates 75 g
- Sugar 35 g
- Protein 2 g
- Cholesterol 0 mg

# SNACKS & APPETIZERS

## 56

## BACON JALAPENO POPPERS

**Preparation Time:** 10 minutes
**Cooking Time:** 30 minutes
**Serve:** 5
**Ingredients:**
- 10 jalapeno peppers, slice lengthwise & remove seeds
- 8 oz cream cheese
- 1 tbsp vinegar
- 1 cup bacon, cooked & chopped
- 1 cup green onion, chopped

**Directions:**
1. Preheat the oven to 375 F.
2. In a bowl, mix bacon, cream cheese, vinegar, and green onion.
3. Stuff bacon mixture into each jalapeno half.
4. Arrange stuffed jalapenos onto the parchment-lined baking pan and bake in a preheated oven for 30 minutes.
5. Serve and enjoy.

**Nutritional Value (Amount per Serving):**
- Calories 267

- Fat 24.8 g
- Carbohydrates 6.6 g
- Sugar 1.5 g
- Protein 7.3 g
- Cholesterol 50 mg

## 57

# PERFECT CRAB DIP

**Preparation Time:** 10 minutes
**Cooking Time:** 20 minutes
**Serve:** 8
**Ingredients:**
- 1 lb crab meat
- ½ tsp pepper
- 1 ½ tbsp lemon juice
- 1 tbsp hot sauce
- 1 tbsp Worcestershire sauce
- 1 garlic clove, minced
- ¼ cup onion, minced
- 1 cup cheddar cheese, grated
- 1 cup pepper jack cheese, grated
- ¼ cup sour cream
- ¼ cup mayonnaise
- 8 oz cream cheese
- ½ tsp kosher salt

**Directions:**
1. Preheat the oven to 325 F.

2.In a bowl, beat sour cream, mayonnaise, and cream cheese until smooth.

3.Add remaining ingredients and mix until well combined.

4.Pour mixture into the baking dish and spread evenly.

5.Place a baking dish onto the oven rack and bake for 20 minutes.

6.Serve with crackers.

**Nutritional Value (Amount per Serving):**
- Calories 256
- Fat 19.6 g
- Carbohydrates 5 g
- Sugar 1.2 g
- Protein 13.2 g
- Cholesterol 81 mg

## 58

## YUMMY CORN DIP

**Preparation Time:** 10 minutes
**Cooking Time:** 20 minutes
**Serve:** 6
**Ingredients:**
- 15 oz can corn kernel, drained
- 1 tbsp green chilies, diced
- 2 green onions, sliced
- ½ bell pepper, diced
- ½ cup cheddar cheese, shredded
- 1 tsp smoked paprika
- ¼ cup sour cream
- 1/3 cup mayonnaise

**Directions:**
1. Preheat the oven to 350 F.
2. Add all ingredients into the mixing bowl and mix until well combined.
3. Pour mixture into the baking dish.
4. Place a baking dish onto the oven rack and bake for 20 minutes.
5. Serve with crackers.

**Nutritional Value (Amount per Serving):**
- Calories 174
- Fat 10.3 g
- Carbohydrates 18.6 g
- Sugar 3.9 g
- Protein 4.9 g
- Cholesterol 18 mg

## 59

## GARLIC CHEESE DIP

**Preparation Time:** 10 minutes
**Cooking Time:** 20 minutes
**Serve:** 6
**Ingredients:**
- 2 cups ricotta cheese
- 1 tsp garlic, minced
- 1/2 cup mozzarella cheese, shredded
- 1 lemon zest
- 3 tbsp olive oil
- 1/4 cup parmesan cheese, shredded
- Pepper
- Salt

**Directions:**
1. Preheat the oven to 375 F.
2. Add all ingredients into the bowl and mix until well combined.
3. Pour mixture into the greased casserole dish.
4. Place the casserole dish onto the oven rack and bake for 20 minutes.
5. Serve and enjoy.

**Nutritional Value (Amount per Serving):**
- Calories 181
- Fat 14 g
- Carbohydrates 4.5 g
- Sugar 0.3 g
- Protein 10.1 g
- Cholesterol 27 mg

## 60

# BAKED POTATO WEDGES

**Preparation Time:** 10 minutes
**Cooking Time:** 15 minutes
**Serve:** 4
**Ingredients:**
- 2 potatoes, cut into wedges
- ½ tsp garlic powder
- ½ tsp paprika
- 1/8 tsp chili powder
- 2 tbsp olive oil
- Salt

**Directions:**
1. Preheat the oven to 350 F.
2. Soak potato wedges in the water for 1 hour. Drain well and pat dry with a paper towel.
3. In a bowl, toss potato wedges with oil, chili powder, paprika, garlic powder, and salt.
4. Spread potato wedges on the parchment-lined baking pan and bake for 15-20 minutes.
5. Serve and enjoy.

**Nutritional Value (Amount per Serving):**

- Calories 136
- Fat 7.2 g
- Carbohydrates 17.2 g
- Sugar 1.4 g
- Protein 1.9 g
- Cholesterol 0 mg

## 61

## HEALTHY VEGETABLE BITES

**Preparation Time:** 10 minutes
**Cooking Time:** 20 minutes
**Serve:** 6
**Ingredients:**
- 1 egg
- 1 cup cooked quinoa
- 2 oz cheddar cheese, shredded
- 2 oz mozzarella cheese, shredded
- 1 cup mixed vegetables, cooked & chopped
- ½ tsp kosher salt

**Directions:**
1. Preheat the oven to 350 F.
2. Spray mini muffin tin with cooking spray and set aside.
3. Add all ingredients to a bowl and mix until well combined.
4. Divide the mixture between the cups of a prepared mini muffin tin, and press down.
5. Place muffin tin onto the oven rack and bake for 20 minutes.
6. Serve and enjoy.

**Nutritional Value (Amount per Serving):**
- Calories 194

- Fat 7.4 g
- Carbohydrates 21.6 g
- Sugar 0.1 g
- Protein 10.5 g
- Cholesterol 42 mg

## 62

# TASTY ROASTED CHICKPEAS

**Preparation Time:** 10 minutes
**Cooking Time:** 30 minutes
**Serve:** 4
**Ingredients:**
- 15 oz can chickpeas, drained & rinsed
- 1 tbsp olive oil
- 1 tsp chili powder
- ¼ tsp pepper
- 1 tsp salt

**Directions:**
1. Preheat the oven to 400 F.
2. Spread chickpeas onto the parchment-lined baking pan and bake for 15 minutes.
3. Remove chickpeas from the oven and place them into the bowl.
4. Add remaining ingredients to the bowl and toss well.
5. Bake chickpeas for 15 minutes more.
6. Serve and enjoy.

**Nutritional Value (Amount per Serving):**
- Calories 159

- Fat 4.8 g
- Carbohydrates 24.5 g
- Sugar 0.1 g
- Protein 5.4 g
- Cholesterol 0 mg

## 63

## CHEESY CAULIFLOWER TOTS

**Preparation Time:** 10 minutes
**Cooking Time:** 25 minutes
**Serve:** 6
**Ingredients:**
- 1 egg
- 2 cups cauliflower florets
- 1/2 cup cheddar cheese, shredded
- 1/4 cup bell pepper, minced
- 1 small onion, minced
- 1/4 cup breadcrumbs
- 1/4 cup parmesan cheese, shredded
- Pepper
- Salt

**Directions:**
1. Preheat the oven to 375 F.
2. Boil cauliflower florets in hot water for 5 minutes.
3. Drain cauliflower and blend in a food processor.
4. Add blended cauliflower and remaining ingredients in bowl and mix until well combined.
5. Make small tots from cauliflower mixture and place onto the

parchment-lined baking pan and bake in preheated oven for 20 minutes. Turn tots halfway through.

6. Serve and enjoy.

**Nutritional Value (Amount per Serving):**
- Calories 95
- Fat 5.1 g
- Carbohydrates 6.8 g
- Sugar 1.9 g
- Protein 6 g
- Cholesterol 40 mg

# DEHYDRATE

## 64

## YELLOW SQUASH CHIPS

**Preparation Time:** 10 minutes
**Cooking Time:** 5 hours
**Serve:** 4
**Ingredients:**
- 4 small yellow squash, cut into 1/8-inch slices
- 1 ½ tsp olive oil
- 1 ½ tsp sea salt

**Directions:**
1. In a bowl, toss squash slices with oil and salt.
2. Place rack onto a baking tray then arrange squash slices onto the rack. Insert into the oven.
3. Press dehydrate mode and set the timer to 5 hours.
4. Store squash chips in an air-tight container.

**Nutritional Value (Amount per Serving):**
- Calories 34
- Fat 2 g
- Carbohydrates 4 g
- Sugar 2 g
- Protein 1.4 g
- Cholesterol 0 mg

## 65

# EGGPLANT CHIPS

**Preparation Time:** 10 minutes
**Cooking Time:** 5 hours
**Serve:** 6
**Ingredients:**
- 4 cups eggplant slices, sliced thinly
- ½ cup parmesan cheese, grated
- 1 tsp Italian seasoning
- ½ cup tomato sauce

**Directions:**
1. Brush eggplant slices with tomato sauce and sprinkle with parmesan cheese and Italian seasoning.
2. Place rack onto a baking tray then arrange eggplant slices onto the rack. Insert into the oven.
3. Press dehydrate mode and set the timer to 5 hours.
4. Store eggplant chips in an air-tight container.

**Nutritional Value (Amount per Serving):**
- Calories 121
- Fat 6.4 g
- Carbohydrates 4.4 g

- Sugar 2.6 g
- Protein 8.8 g
- Cholesterol 21 mg

## 66

# KIWI CHIPS

**Preparation Time:** 10 minutes
**Cooking Time:** 5 hours
**Serve:** 6
**Ingredients:**
- 6 kiwis, peel & cut into ¼-inch slices

**Directions:**
1. Place rack onto a baking tray then arrange kiwi slices onto the rack. Insert into the oven.
2. Press dehydrate mode and set the timer to 5 hours.
3. Store kiwi chips in an air-tight container.

**Nutritional Value (Amount per Serving):**
- Calories 46
- Fat 0.4 g
- Carbohydrates 11.1 g
- Sugar 6.8 g
- Protein 0.9 g
- Cholesterol 0 mg

## 67

# KALE CHIPS

**Preparation Time:** 10 minutes
**Cooking Time:** 2 hours
**Serve:** 6
**Ingredients:**
- 3 bunches kale, remove stem & cut into bite-size pieces
- 1 tbsp olive oil
- 1 ½ tsp garlic powder
- 3 ½ tbsp nutritional yeast
- 1 tsp salt

**Directions:**
1. Add kale into the large bowl.
2. Add oil, garlic powder, and salt over the kale and mix well.
3. Sprinkle with nutritional yeast and toss well.
4. Place rack onto a baking tray then arrange kale pieces onto the rack. Insert into the oven.
5. Press dehydrate mode and set the timer to 2 hours.
6. Store kale chips in an air-tight container.

**Nutritional Value (Amount per Serving):**
- Calories 59

- Fat 2.7 g
- Carbohydrates 6.7 g
- Sugar 0.2 g
- Protein 3.8 g
- Cholesterol 0 mg

## 68

# ZUCCHINI CHIPS

**Preparation Time:** 10 minutes
**Cooking Time:** 5 hours
**Serve:** 4
**Ingredients:**
- 2 zucchini, sliced thinly
- ¼ tsp smoked paprika
- ¼ tsp chili powder
- Salt

**Directions:**

1. Add zucchini slices, smoked paprika, chili powder, and salt into the bowl and toss well.

2. Place rack onto a baking tray then arrange zucchini slices onto the rack. Insert into the oven.

3. Press dehydrate mode and set the timer to 5 hours.

4. Store zucchini chips in an air-tight container.

**Nutritional Value (Amount per Serving):**
- Calories 17
- Fat 0.2 g
- Carbohydrates 3.4 g

- Sugar 1.7 g
- Protein 1.2 g
- Cholesterol 0 mg

## 69

## BANANA SLICES

**Preparation Time:** 10 minutes
**Cooking Time:** 5 hours
**Serve:** 4
**Ingredients:**
- 4 bananas, peel & cut into 1/8-inch slices

**Directions:**
1. Place rack onto a baking tray then arrange banana slices onto the rack. Insert into the oven.
2. Press dehydrate mode and set the timer to 5 hours.
3. Store banana slices in an air-tight container.

**Nutritional Value (Amount per Serving):**
- Calories 105
- Fat 0.4 g
- Carbohydrates 27 g
- Sugar 14.4 g
- Protein 1.3 g
- Cholesterol 0 mg

## 70

# PEAR SLICES

**Preparation Time:** 10 minutes
**Cooking Time:** 5 hours
**Serve:** 4
**Ingredients:**
- 4 pears, cut into ¼-inch thick slices

**Directions:**
1. Place rack onto a baking tray then arrange pear slices onto the rack. Insert into the oven.
2. Press dehydrate mode and set the timer to 5 hours.
3. Store pear slices in an air-tight container.

**Nutritional Value (Amount per Serving):**
- Calories 121
- Fat 0.3 g
- Carbohydrates 31.8 g
- Sugar 20.4 g
- Protein 0.8 g
- Cholesterol 0 mg

## 71

# SALMON JERKY

**Preparation Time:** 10 minutes
**Cooking Time:** 4 hours
**Serve:** 6
**Ingredients:**
- 1 lb salmon, cut into ¼-inch slices
- 6 tbsp soy sauce
- ¾ tbsp molasses
- 1 tbsp fresh lemon juice
- ½ tsp liquid smoke

**Directions:**

1. Add salmon slices, soy sauce, liquid smoke, lemon juice, molasses, and soy sauce into the zip-lock bag, seal bag shake well and place in the refrigerator for overnight.

2. Remove salmon slices from marinade.

3. Place rack onto a baking tray then arrange salmon slices onto the rack. Insert into the oven.

4. Press dehydrate mode and set the timer to 4 hours.

**Nutritional Value (Amount per Serving):**
- Calories 116

- Fat 4.7 g
- Carbohydrates 3.1 g
- Sugar 1.7 g
- Protein 15.7 g
- Cholesterol 33 mg

# DESSERTS

## 72

## DELICIOUS PINEAPPLE BARS

**Preparation Time:** 10 minutes
**Cooking Time:** 35 minutes
**Serve:** 12
**Ingredients:**
- 2 eggs
- 1 ¼ cup crushed pineapple, drained
- ¼ tsp baking soda
- 1 cup all-purpose flour
- 1 cup sugar
- ½ cup butter, softened
- Pinch of salt

**Directions:**
1. Preheat the oven to 350 F.
2. Spray 9*9-inch baking pan with cooking spray and set aside.
3. In a mixing bowl, mix together eggs, sugar, and butter.
4. Add baking soda, flour, and salt and beat until well combined.
5. Add crushed pineapple and stir well.
6. Pour mixture into the prepared baking pan.

7. Place the baking pan onto the oven rack and bake for 35 minutes.

8. Remove from the oven and let it cool for 10 minutes.

9. Cut into pieces and serve.

**Nutritional Value (Amount per Serving):**
- Calories 187
- Fat 8.5 g
- Carbohydrates 27 g
- Sugar 18.5 g
- Protein 2.2 g
- Cholesterol 48 mg

## 73

## CINNAMON HONEY PEARS

**Preparation Time:** 10 minutes
**Cooking Time:** 30 minutes
**Serve:** 4
**Ingredients:**
- 4 pears, peel, cut in half & scoop out & core
- ½ tsp vanilla
- ½ tsp ground cinnamon
- 2 tbsp butter, melted
- 3 tbsp honey

**Directions:**
1. Preheat the oven to 400 F.
2. Place pears in a 9*13-inch baking dish.
3. In a small bowl, mix honey, melted butter, cinnamon, and vanilla.
4. Pour honey mixture over pears.
5. Place baking dish onto the oven rack and bake for 30 minutes.
6. Remove from the oven and let it cool for 5-10 minutes.
7. Serve and enjoy.

**Nutritional Value (Amount per Serving):**

- Calories 222
- Fat 6.1 g
- Carbohydrates 45.1 g
- Sugar 33.4 g
- Protein 0.9 g
- Cholesterol 15 mg

## 74

# CINNAMON APPLE SLICES

**Preparation Time:** 10 minutes
**Cooking Time:** 30 minutes
**Serve:** 4
**Ingredients:**
- 3 apples, cut into ½-inch thick wedges
- 1/3 cup butter, melted
- ½ tsp ground cinnamon
- 2 tbsp brown sugar

**Directions:**
1. Preheat the oven to 350 F.
2. Add apple slices into the large mixing bowl.
3. In a small bowl, mix brown sugar, melted butter, and cinnamon until sugar is dissolved.
4. Pour sugar mixture over apple slices and mix until well coated.
5. Pour apple slices into the baking dish.
6. Place baking dish onto the oven rack and bake for 30 minutes. Stir apple slices after every 10 minutes.
7. Serve baked apple slices with vanilla ice-cream.

**Nutritional Value (Amount per Serving):**

- Calories 240
- Fat 15.7 g
- Carbohydrates 27.8 g
- Sugar 21.8 g
- Protein 0.6 g
- Cholesterol 41 mg

## 75

# MOIST YOGURT CAKE

**Preparation Time:** 10 minutes
**Cooking Time:** 40 minutes
**Serve:** 8
**Ingredients:**
- 2 eggs
- 2 cups all-purpose flour
- 1 cup plain yogurt
- 1 lemon zest
- ½ tsp vanilla
- 2 tsp baking powder
- ½ cup canola oil
- ½ cup sugar
- 3 tbsp orange jam
- Pinch of salt

**Directions:**
1. Preheat the oven to 350 F.
2. Grease 9.5*2.5-inch loaf pan and set aside.
3. Add eggs, yogurt, vanilla, lemon zest, oil, and sugar in mixing bowl and beat until smooth.

4. Add baking powder, flour, and salt and mix until just combined.

5. Pour batter into the prepared loaf pan.

6. Place loaf pan onto the oven rack and bake for 35-40 minutes.

7. Remove loaf pan from the oven and let it cool for 10 minutes.

8. Spread orange jam on top of the cake.

9. Slice and serve.

**Nutritional Value (Amount per Serving):**
- Calories 321
- Fat 15.4 g
- Carbohydrates 39.2 g
- Sugar 14.9 g
- Protein 6.4 g
- Cholesterol 43 mg

## 76

## EASY BLONDE BROWNIE

**Preparation Time:** 10 minutes
**Cooking Time:** 20 minutes
**Serve:** 8
**Ingredients:**
- 2 eggs
- ½ cup chocolate chips
- 2 cup all-purpose flour
- 2 tsp baking powder
- 1 ½ tsp vanilla
- 1 ¼ cup brown sugar
- 1 cup butter, melted
- ½ tsp salt

**Directions:**
1. Preheat the oven to 350 F.
2. Grease 9*13-inch baking pan and set aside.
3. In a mixing bowl, mix melted butter and sugar. Add vanilla and eggs and mix well.
4. Add flour, baking powder, and salt and mix until well combined.
5. Add chocolate chips and stir well.

6. Pour batter into the prepared pan and spread evenly.

7. Place the baking pan onto the oven rack and bake for 20 minutes.

8. Remove from the oven and let it cool completely.

9. Slice and serve.

**Nutritional Value (Amount per Serving):**
- Calories 479
- Fat 27.5 g
- Carbohydrates 53.1 g
- Sugar 27.7 g
- Protein 5.7 g
- Cholesterol 104 mg

## 77

# FUDGY CHOCOLATE BROWNIES

**Preparation Time:** 10 minutes
**Cooking Time:** 20 minutes
**Serve:** 16
**Ingredients:**
- 2 eggs
- ½ cup flour
- 1 tsp vanilla
- 1 cup sugar
- ½ cup cocoa powder
- ½ cup butter, melted
- ¼ tsp salt

**Directions:**
1. Preheat the oven to 350 F.
2. Grease 8*8-inch pan and set aside.
3. In a bowl, mix cocoa powder and melted butter. Add sugar and stir until dissolved.
4. Add vanilla and eggs and mix until well combined.
5. Add flour and salt and stir until combine.
6. Pour batter in prepared pan and spread evenly.
7. Place the pan onto the oven rack and bake for 20 minutes.

8. Remove from the oven and let it cool completely.
9. Slice and serve.

**Nutritional Value (Amount per Serving):**
- Calories 127
- Fat 6.7 g
- Carbohydrates 17 g
- Sugar 12.6 g
- Protein 1.6 g
- Cholesterol 36 mg

## 78

# SOFT & MOIST LEMON BROWNIES

**Preparation Time:** 10 minutes
**Cooking Time:** 20 minutes
**Serve:** 16
**Ingredients:**
- 2 eggs
- ½ tsp baking powder
- ¾ cup all-purpose flour
- 1 tbsp fresh lemon juice
- ½ lemon zest
- ¾ cup sugar
- ½ cup butter, softened

**Directions:**
1. Preheat the oven to 350 F.
2. Grease 8*8-inch pan and set aside.
3. In a large bowl, beat sugar, butter, and lemon zest until fluffy.
4. Add eggs, lemon juice, and flour and mix until combined.
5. Pour batter into the prepared pan and spread evenly.
6. Place the pan onto the oven rack and bake for 20 minutes.
7. Remove from the oven and let it cool completely.

8. Slice and serve.

**Nutritional Value (Amount per Serving):**
- Calories 116
- Fat 6.4 g
- Carbohydrates 14 g
- Sugar 9.5 g
- Protein 1.4 g
- Cholesterol 36 mg

## 79

## EASY LEMON COOKIES

**Preparation Time:** 10 minutes
**Cooking Time:** 11 minutes
**Serve:** 12
**Ingredients:**
- 1 egg yolk
- ½ tsp baking powder
- ¼ tsp baking soda
- 1 lemon zest
- 2 tsp vanilla
- 1 tbsp brown sugar
- 1 cup sugar
- 1 ¼ cups flour
- ½ cup butter, softened
- ¼ tsp salt

**Directions:**
1. Preheat the oven to 350 F.
2. In a bowl, mix flour, baking powder, baking soda, and salt.
3. In a separate bowl, beat butter, ¾ cup sugar, and brown sugar until fluffy.

4. Add eggs, vanilla, and lemon zest and beat until just combined.

5. Slowly add flour mixture and mix until just combined.

6. Make 1 ½-inch ball from mixture and roll into the remaining sugar and place onto the parchment-lined baking pan.

7. Bake in preheated oven for 11 minutes.

8. Remove from the oven and let it cool completely.

9. Serve and enjoy.

**Nutritional Value (Amount per Serving):**
- Calories 187
- Fat 8.2 g
- Carbohydrates 27.6 g
- Sugar 17.6 g
- Protein 1.7 g
- Cholesterol 38 mg

## 80

## CHOCOLATE CHIP COOKIES

**Preparation Time:** 10 minutes
**Cooking Time:** 8 minutes
**Serve:** 30
**Ingredients:**
- 1 egg
- 12 oz chocolate chips
- 2 cups self-rising flour
- ½ cup brown sugar
- 2/3 cup sugar
- 1 tsp vanilla
- 1 cup butter, softened

**Directions:**
1. Preheat the oven to 375 F.
2. In a bowl, mix egg, vanilla, and butter.
3. Add brown sugar and sugar and beat until creamy.
4. Slowly add flour and mix until just combined.
5. Add chocolate chips and stir well.
6. Spoon out cookie dough onto the parchment-lined baking pan.
7. Bake in preheated oven for 8-10 minutes.

8. Remove from the oven and let it cool completely.
9. Serve and enjoy.

**Nutritional Value (Amount per Serving):**
- Calories 174
- Fat 9.7 g
- Carbohydrates 19.9 g
- Sugar 12.7 g
- Protein 2 g
- Cholesterol 24 mg

# 30-DAY MEAL PLAN

**Day 1**
    Breakfast- Apple Oat Cups
    Lunch-Spinach Zucchini Casserole
    Dinner- Smoked Paprika Pork Chops

**Day 2**
    Breakfast- Spinach Tomato Egg Muffins
    Lunch-Zucchini Potato Gratin
    Dinner-Beef Zucchini Burger Patties

**Day 3**
    Breakfast- Perfect Potato Casserole
    Lunch-Zucchini Tomato Bake
    Dinner-Greek Lamb Patties

**Day 4**
    Breakfast- Ham Cheese Casserole
    Lunch-Blackened Fish Fillets
    Dinner-Rosemary Pork Chops

**Day 5**
    Breakfast- Fluffy Breakfast Egg Muffins
    Lunch-Easy Brown Sugar Chicken
    Dinner-Juicy Pork Tenderloin

**Day 6**
Breakfast- Pumpkin Bread
Lunch-Garlic Butter Shrimp
Dinner- Baked Pork Ribs
**Day 7**
Breakfast- Healthy Banana Bread
Lunch-Simple Cajun Salmon
Dinner- Rosemary Pork Chops
**Day 8**
Breakfast- Baked Oatmeal
Lunch-Creamy Chicken
Dinner-Baked Pork Patties
**Day 9**
Breakfast- Healthy Oat Muffins
Lunch-Delicious Turkey Cutlets
Dinner-Pork Chops with Potatoes
**Day 10**
Breakfast- Baked Cinnamon Oatmeal
Lunch-Sweet Dijon Salmon
Dinner-Quick Ranch Pork Chops
**Day 11**
Breakfast- Apple Oat Cups
Lunch-Flavorful Shrimp Fajitas
Dinner- Simple Spiced Pork Chops
**Day 12**
Breakfast- Spinach Tomato Egg Muffins
Lunch-Flavors Catfish Fillets
Dinner-Beef Onion Bake
**Day 13**
Breakfast- Perfect Potato Casserole
Lunch-Delicious Pesto Salmon
Dinner- Pork Chops with Potatoes
**Day 14**
Breakfast- Ham Cheese Casserole
Lunch-Turkey Spinach Patties
Dinner- Rosemary Pork Chops

**Day 15**
Breakfast- Fluffy Breakfast Egg Muffins
Lunch-Juicy Chicken Drumsticks
Dinner- Beef Zucchini Burger Patties
**Day 16**
Breakfast- Apple Oat Cups
Lunch-Spinach Zucchini Casserole
Dinner- Smoked Paprika Pork Chops
**Day 17**
Breakfast- Spinach Tomato Egg Muffins
Lunch-Zucchini Potato Gratin
Dinner-Beef Zucchini Burger Patties
**Day 18**
Breakfast- Perfect Potato Casserole
Lunch-Zucchini Tomato Bake
Dinner-Greek Lamb Patties
**Day 19**
Breakfast- Ham Cheese Casserole
Lunch-Blackened Fish Fillets
Dinner-Rosemary Pork Chops
**Day 20**
Breakfast- Fluffy Breakfast Egg Muffins
Lunch-Easy Brown Sugar Chicken
Dinner-Juicy Pork Tenderloin
**Day 21**
Breakfast- Pumpkin Bread
Lunch-Garlic Butter Shrimp
Dinner- Baked Pork Ribs
**Day 22**
Breakfast- Healthy Banana Bread
Lunch-Simple Cajun Salmon
Dinner- Rosemary Pork Chops
**Day 23**
Breakfast- Baked Oatmeal
Lunch-Creamy Chicken
Dinner-Baked Pork Patties

**Day 24**
Breakfast- Healthy Oat Muffins
Lunch-Delicious Turkey Cutlets
Dinner-Pork Chops with Potatoes
**Day 25**
Breakfast- Baked Cinnamon Oatmeal
Lunch-Sweet Dijon Salmon
Dinner-Quick Ranch Pork Chops
**Day 26**
Breakfast- Apple Oat Cups
Lunch-Flavorful Shrimp Fajitas
Dinner- Simple Spiced Pork Chops
**Day 27**
Breakfast- Spinach Tomato Egg Muffins
Lunch-Flavors Catfish Fillets
Dinner-Beef Onion Bake
**Day 28**
Breakfast- Perfect Potato Casserole
Lunch-Delicious Pesto Salmon
Dinner- Pork Chops with Potatoes
**Day 29**
Breakfast- Ham Cheese Casserole
Lunch-Turkey Spinach Patties
Dinner- Rosemary Pork Chops
**Day 30**
Breakfast- Fluffy Breakfast Egg Muffins
Lunch-Juicy Chicken Drumsticks
Dinner- Beef Zucchini Burger Patties

# CONCLUSION

The Oster Digital French door oven is one of the best innovative convection ovens loaded with turbo convection technology which makes your daily cooking process faster. The Oster oven is perfect kitchen appliances capable to handle multiple tasks into single appliances. A digital touch control panel helps you to perform different cooking tasks like Bake, Broil, Toast, Warm, Pizza, Defrost, and Dehydrate.

The Oster Digital French door oven cookbook contains 80 delicious and healthy recipes written from breakfast to desserts. All the recipes written in this cookbook are selected from globally inspired dishes and written into an easily understandable form. The recipes in this book are given with their perfect preparation and cooking time. Each and every recipe ends with their nutritional value information.

www.ingramcontent.com/pod-product-compliance
Lightning Source LLC
Chambersburg PA
CBHW071619080526
44588CB00010B/1190